Noah's Ark
With Press-Out Ark, Animals, People & More

Retold and illustrated
by
Michael Evans

Ideals Children's Books • Nashville, Tennessee

Copyright © 1993 by Michael Evans
All rights reserved.

Published by Ideals Publishing Corporation
Nashville, Tennessee 37214

Printed and bound in the United States of America.

Created and designed by Treld Bicknell.

ISBN 0-8249-8600-8

Long after God created the earth and all living things, He saw that His people had become wicked. They fought, robbed, and killed one another.

God grew sorry that He had made people, and His heart filled with pain. He decided to destroy all living things under the skies—man and beast, birds and creeping things.

All except Noah—a good man who lived at peace with God. Noah had three sons: Shem, Ham, and Japheth.

God spoke to Noah and said, "The people of the earth have become wicked. I am going to destroy them and the land in which they live.

"Build an ark of gopher wood," God instructed Noah, "with three stories of rooms inside. Build it 450 feet long, seventy-five feet wide, and forty-five feet tall.

"Coat the ark with tar inside and out, build a roof on top, and put a door in its side. Make it strong and secure.

"I will bring a flood of waters upon the earth," God explained. "Everything on earth will die. But I will make a covenant with you, a promise that will last forever.

"You and your wife, and your sons and their wives, must go into the ark—you are good and I want you to be safe. And you must take two of every living creature, one male and one female, to keep them alive.

"Gather all the different foods that are eaten, and take them into the ark as food for you and for the animals."

And Noah did all that the Lord commanded.

After seven days, the flood of waters came upon the earth. On that same day, Noah and his wife, and his sons and their wives, entered the ark. Every beast and every bird, every insect and every creeping thing came to Noah and entered the ark. They went in two by two, just as God had commanded—and when the last creature had entered, God shut them in.

The rain came down for forty days and forty nights. The waters grew deeper and lifted up the ark until it was floating high above the ground.

The waters rose higher and higher until the hills and the mountains were covered. The ark drifted upon the water.

Just as God had said, every living thing on the earth died—all of the animals and all of the people. Only Noah and those with him in the ark remained alive.

The waters flooded the earth for 150 days. But God remembered Noah and all that waited with him in the ark. Soon God sent a strong wind over the earth to help dry up the land. The rain stopped and the flood waters went down.

The ark came to rest upon the mountains of Ararat. And the waters continued to go down until the tops of the mountains were seen.

After many days, Noah opened the window of the ark and sent out a raven. The raven flew in search of dry land, but it could find none. Then Noah sent a dove out. But the dove could not find a place to rest, and it returned to the ark.

Noah waited seven days and sent the dove out again. When the dove returned with an olive leaf in its beak, Noah said, "There must be dry land." Still they waited.

Once more Noah sent the dove out—this time it did not return. Noah knew that the flood was gone from the earth.

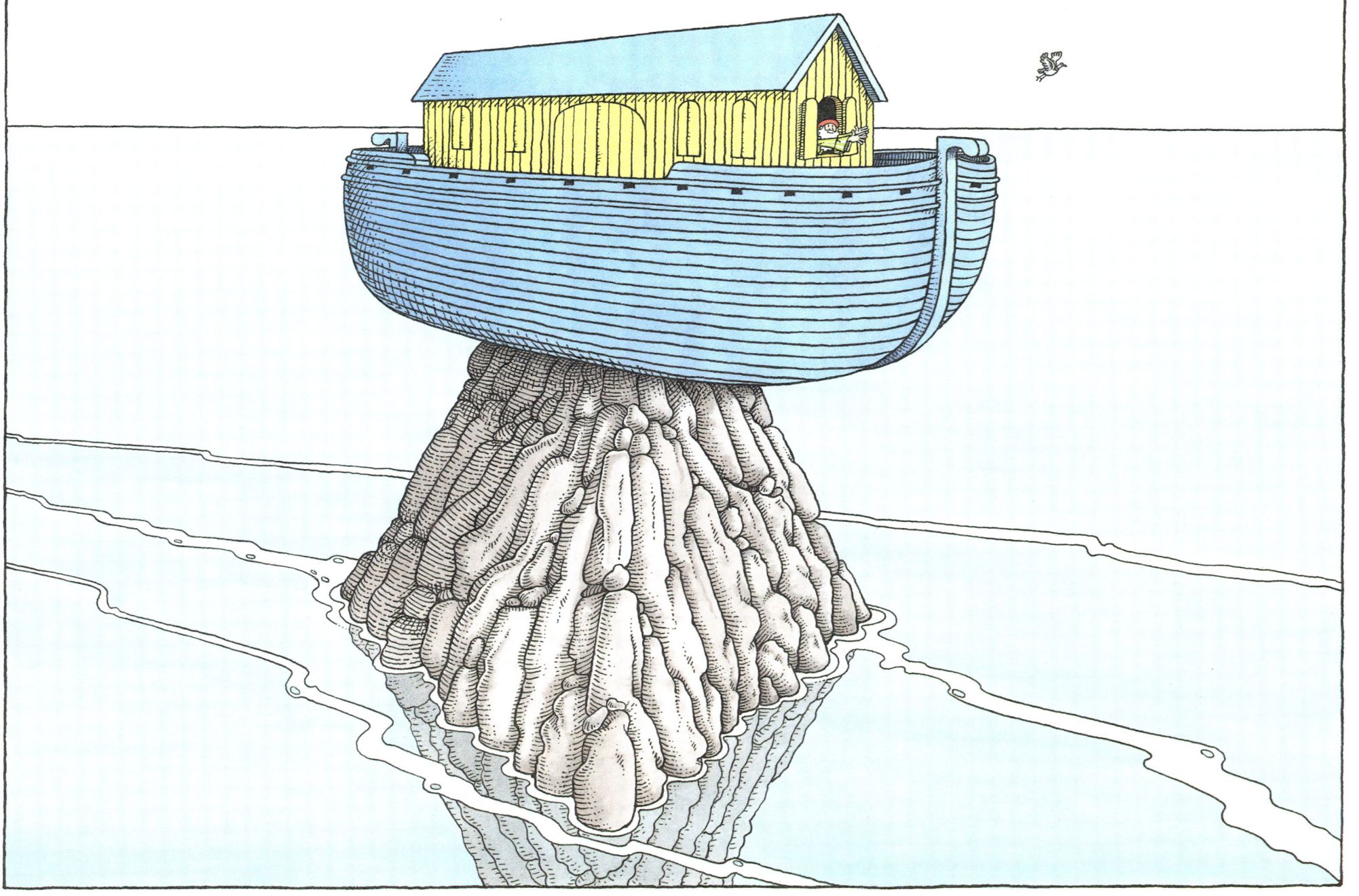

Noah looked out from the ark and saw that the face of the ground was dry. And God said to Noah, "Go out of the ark, and your wife, and your sons and their wives with you. Bring out every living creature that is on the ark, so that they may make new families and fill the earth again."

So Noah left the ark with his wife and his sons and their wives. Every living thing—every beast and every bird, every insect and every creeping thing—went out of the ark.

Then Noah built an altar and gave thanks to God.

God was pleased. He blessed Noah and his family and said to them, "Have many children and fill the earth with people once more." Then God made His covenant. He said, "I promise never again to bring a flood upon the earth to destroy all the living things."

Then God set a rainbow in the sky, saying, "This is a sign of my covenant with you and all living creatures. Whenever I bring a cloud over the earth and the rainbow appears in the sky, I will remember my promise. And you will know that my promise will last forever."